Dog Chinese Horoscope 2024

By
IChingHun FengShuisu

Copyright © 2024 By IChingHun FengShuisu
All rights reserved

Table of Contents

Introduce 5
Year of the DOG (Fire) | (1946) & (2006) 8
    Overview 8
    Career and Business 9
    Financial 10
    Family 11
    Love 12
    Health 13
Year of the DOG (Earth) | (1958) 15
    Overview 15
    Career and Business 16
    Financial 17
    Family 18
    Love 19
    Health 20
Year of the DOG (Gold) | (1970) 21
    Overview 21
    Career and Business 22
    Financial 24
    Family 25
    Love 26
    Health 27
Year of the DOG (Water) | (1982) 28
    Overview 28
    Career and Business 29
    Financial 30
    Family 31

Love 32

　　Health 33

Year of the DOG (Wood) | (1994) 34

　　Overview 34

　　Career and Business 35

　　Financial 36

　　Family 37

　　Love 38

　　Health 39

Chinese Astrology Horoscope for Each Month 40

　　Month 12 in the Rabbit Year (6 Jan 23 - 3 Feb 23) 40

　　Month 1 in the Dragon Year (4 Feb 23 - 5 Mar 23) 42

　　Month 2 in the Dragon Year (6 Mar 23 - 5 Apr 23) 44

　　Month 3 in the Dragon Year (6 Apr 23 - 5 May 23) 46

　　Month 4 in the Dragon Year (6 May 23 - 5 Jun 23) 48

　　Month 5 in the Dragon Year (6 Jun 23 - 6 Jul 23) 51

　　Month 6 in the Dragon Year (7 Jul 23 - 7 Aug 23) 53

　　Month 7 in the Dragon Year (8 Aug 23 - 7 Sep 23) 55

　　Month 8 in the Dragon Year (8 Sep 23 - 7 Oct 23) 57

　　Month 9 in the Dragon Year (8 Oct 23 - 6 Nov 23) 60

　　Month 10 in the Dragon Year (7 Nov 23 - 6 Dec 23) 62

　　Month 11 in the Dragon Year (7 Dec 23 - 5 Jan 24) 64

Amulet for The Year of the Dog 68

Introduce

The character of people born in the year of the DOG

People born in the Year of the Dog are good people who are honest, trustworthy, and considerate when others ask for assistance. You are sincere, open, honest, and tenacious. But he is never selfish; he always thinks of others first. The heart is filled with love and virtue, and it is ready to fight for the rights of both oneself and others. It is usually very gentle when it comes to manners. However, it is concealed by a distorted ax-like character. You are a loyal companion despite being angry and irritable with your friends. Be sincere and do not betray those who have placed their trust in you.

Strength:

You are always up to date on events, have a keen understanding of the situation, and never abandon your friends in difficult times.

Weaknesses:
You are overly concerned with the affairs of others, which makes it easy for you to get into trouble.

Love:
People born in the Year of the Dog are unafraid of silent love. Maybe we've known each other for almost a year. Nobody knows at work. The secret is broken when you become involved with someone until someone secretly sees you. People born this year are quiet people who enjoy solitude but have a quiet demeanor. I'll tell you that love affairs will not be easy on your love story. People born in the Year of the Dog experience chaos as well. This type of lust results from being careless and not being afraid to sacrifice yourself. I just want to have fun sometimes, but withdrawing is also difficult.
When there is a lover as a person, the people of the Year of the Dog will stop all flirting and immediately turn to love and love.

Suitable Career:
People born in the Year of the Dog are classified as earth elemental. As a result, suitable occupations are primarily related to land or land, such as real estate work, land trades, photography, and welding. Selling electrical appliances, restaurants, beauty salons, mining - stone. Agriculture in all forms or doing business with agricultural products as a component, such as baking, processed fruit, ceramics, and pottery. Consultants in construction materials, banking, finance, and securities Selling paper machines to pay homage to the gods, performing government service, and so on.

Year of the DOG (Wood) | (1934) & (1994)

"The DOG on Mountain." is a person born in the year of the DOG at the age of 90 years (1934) and 30 years (1994)

Overview

Destiny, the senior, is 90 years old. This year, you must use greater caution. Because your destiny is in direct conflict with the Year of the Dragon. He also requested the Tai Suai deity and an evil star was orbiting him to destroy him. As a result, various disputes and disruptions will arise, disturbing your thinking. You should also focus more on your own physical and mental well-being. Be cautious of some statements that may offend your children or anyone close to you. It will lead to misunderstandings and arguments at home.

The planets that affect your life cycle this year for the 30 year old horoscope. Dao Sung Mung here. (Sorrow's Star) Furthermore, the year of his birth coincides with the annual confrontation with the Thai Buddha. As a result, every task must be carried out calmly.

You should also be wary of pals who frequently ask you to lose. Be wary about investing and getting duped.

Career and Business

You should be very attentive in your job this year and always endeavor to increase your work efficiency. As a result, always expand your knowledge, improve yourself, and address any evident deficiencies that may damage your commercial enterprise. Because clients may be taken away, you must be vigilant to look at the overall picture of regular inspections and visit customers more frequently. During the months that trade work often encounters obstacles, including the 3rd Chinese month (4 Apr. - 4 May), the 6th Chinese month (6 Jul. - 6 Aug.), the 8th Chinese month (7 Sep. - 7 Oct.), and the 10th Chinese month (7 Nov. - 5 Dec.). Furthermore, you must be cautious of being duped by fraudsters who will take advantage of you, and you must exercise caution while signing contract paperwork. You will be at a disadvantage. More vigilance is required while participating in joint ventures this year since there is a risk of being duped into losing money or discovering insiders or unscrupulous partners harboring frauds. As for the months when your work and business will turn around and get better, they include 1st Chinese month (4 Feb. - 4 Mar.), the 2nd Chinese month (5 Mar. - 3 Apr. .), the 5th Chinese month (5 June - 5 July) and the 9th Chinese month (8 Oct. - 6 Nov.).

Financial

This year's earnings are not promising financially. If you are not fiscally responsible. You cannot avoid the risk of having money in your pocket in the middle of the year. Because you are going to be cash-strapped at work or because your subordinates committed blunders. During the months when your financial criteria will be very difficult, they include the 3rd Chinese month (4 Apr. - 4 May.), the 6th Chinese month (6 Jul. - 6 Aug.), the 8th Chinese month (7 Sep. - 7 Oct.) and the 10th Chinese month (7 Nov. - 5 Dec.), As a result, gambling is outlawed. Even if you can play, money will pass through your hands to briefly make you happy. They will eventually be given more than they received. As a result, please keep your heart in check and don't expect to get rich quickly. Don't expect to keep going till you're dizzy. Because there is nothing except loss and loss. Furthermore, you should not rely on others to sign a promise or to vouch for somebody. Avoiding engagement and investment in unlawful commerce is one example. There will always be problems. For the months when your finances are flowing smoothly, they are: the 1st Chinese month (4 Feb. - 4 Mar.), the 2nd Chinese month (5 Mar. - 3 Apr.), the 5th Chinese month (5 Jun. – 5 Jul.) and the 9th Chinese month (8 Oct. – 6 Nov.)

Family

The family horoscope for this year is not favorable. Because three terrible stars were aiming to destroy them in this fatal situation: the Puenium star, the Sung Miang star, and the Suai Pua star. This will expand its impact, resulting in stories of pain and anguish, potentially even to the point of grieving for the adults who are close to them. There will also be mishaps in the house. To get rid of bad luck and address the situation, you should make time at the start of the year to pay reverence to the Tai Suai deity. You will be able to change terrible things into good. Especially during the months when the family will experience a lot of problems, including the 3rd Chinese month (4 Apr. - 4 May.), the 6th Chinese month (6 Jul. - 6 Aug.), the 8th Chinese month (7 Sep. - 7 Oct.) and the 10th Chinese month (7 Nov. - 5 Dec.) You should examine and maintain any equipment or accessories that might endanger family members. This includes being cautious with important possessions. Be wary of criminals and con artists.

Love
This year's love destiny is a mixed bag of good and evil. Keep in mind that misconceptions might lead to the end of a relationship. As a result, if there is an issue, you should turn around swiftly and alter your knowledge. Don't let minor issues become major ones. Especially during the months that you should support your love well, including the 3rd Chinese

month (4 Apr. - 4 May.), the 6th Chinese month (6 Jul. - 6 Aug.), the 8th Chinese month (7 Sep. - 7 Oct.) and the 10th Chinese month (7 Nov. - 5 Dec.) You should avoid emotional phrases that would influence the other person's emotions and put pressure on you, and you should maintain your commitments. You already said that you should avoid visiting entertainment establishments. As an added benefit, keep an eye out for sexually transmitted illnesses.

Health

His health will be fine this year, but he will face illnesses and injuries. The elder must exercise caution due to his heart, knee, and bone problems. Take care not to slip. Accidents while traveling will result in long-term sleepovers. As a result, you should get enough rest, visit a doctor regularly for annual health checks, and seek medical attention if you notice anything unusual or have symptoms that are not normal. Months in which you need to be careful of health problems and pay special attention to 3rd month of China (5 Apr. - 5 May), 6th month of China (7 Jul. - 7 Aug.), 8th month of China (8

Sep. – 7 Oct.) and 10th month of China (7 Nov. – 6 Dec.) should take care of strict hygiene in eating and living. Beware of gastritis, intestinal disease, esophageal disease, and bronchitis.

Year of the DOG (Fire) | (1946) & (1994)

"The DOG kept to guard private property." is a person born in the year of the DOG at the age of 78 years (1934) and 18 years (2006)

Overview

This life cycle is for people born in the Year of the Dog since your life cycle is a direct birth year. You also disagree with Thep Tai Suea Ia's stance. As a result, every work activity this year will make you more tired than others. Furthermore, one cannot be careless or reckless when performing various activities. This year, you must be wary of minors or those close to you instigating issues. Both meet the requirements for being slandered and causing issues. Furthermore, you should be aware of any safety issues and illnesses that may impact individuals in your house. It is because three wicked stars will radiate from the house of destiny, namely Dao Sung Mueng (star of sadness), Dao Pue Niam (star of wind), and Dao Ung Huang (star of evil). This effect enables you to confront several things at once when you endure tragedy, and what you wish for may go wrong, be betrayed, lose your reputation, or lose money. Furthermore, you must be cautious of health issues, including harm from accidents.

Because the planet that orbits and impacts their age cycle is Puenium, teens around the age of 18 must be cautious of unanticipated risks that may occur from negligence. Outdoor activities must be performed with caution or risk injury. This includes being cautious about mishaps caused by tools, appliances, or other equipment. Be cautious, as there is a risk of bleeding. This includes driving a car. The period comprises the 3rd Chinese month (4 Apr. - 4 May.), the 6th Chinese month (6 Jul. - 6 Aug.), the 8th Chinese month (7 Sep. - 7 Oct.), and the 10th Chinese month (7 Nov. - 5 Dec.).

Career and Business
Monsoons need extra patience, focus, and persistence this year, whether at work or in school. Teenagers can consult with their elders to take particular measures if certain issues cannot be resolved on their own. You should learn the task from an experienced worker.

Seniors must be wary of being cheated or bribed by juniors or subordinates. Especially during the months when work is in decline, including the 3rd Chinese month (4 Apr. - 4 May), the 6th Chinese month (6 Jul. - 6 Aug.), the 8th Chinese month (7 Sep. – 7 Oct.), and the 10th month of China (7 Nov. – 5 Dec.) If there is a criterion, a contract must be signed. Be wary of contracts that take advantage, or you may be duped by crooks. Furthermore, you must be extra cautious when joining joint ventures or investing in other industries. As for the months in which work and studies will see progress and prosperity, they include 1st Chinese month (Feb. 4 - March 4), the 2nd Chinese month (5 Mar - 3 Apr), the 5th Chinese month (5 Jun. – 5 Jul.) and 9th Chinese month (8 Oct. – 6 Nov.)

Financial

The financial fortunes of this year reflect a lack of solid revenue. Income is decreasing, while costs are increasing. During some times, you must be cautious of unforeseen current costs, which might cause you to run out of money. Be wary of cash outflows caused by poor investing decisions.

Especially during the months when the financial stars are down, namely the 3rd Chinese month (4 Apr. - 4 May), the 6th Chinese month (6 Jul. - 6 Aug.), the 8th Chinese month (7 Sep. – 7 Oct.), and the 10th Chinese month (7 Nov. – 5 Dec.) Do not invest in illegal businesses, do not gamble, gamble, do not lend money to others, or sign financial guarantees. As for the months with good financial luck and prosperity, they are the 1st Chinese month (4 Feb. - 4 Mar.), the 2nd Chinese month (5 Mar. - 3 Apr.), the 5th Chinese month (5 Jun. – 5 Jul.) and the 9th Chinese month (8 Oct. – 6 Nov.).

Family

The discovery of an evil star targeting and pestering you has resulted in this year's family horoscope. As a result, disturbance incidents are common outside. Be cautious when grieving over elderly relatives. Both should be cautious regarding home safety and mishaps. In many situations, family and friends might be difficult to trust and rely on, resulting in turmoil and confusion for relatives and friends. This year, say little and don't inform anyone until it's gone. Because you may be the victim of some ill-wishers looking for a method to take advantage of you. Also, stay out of your friends' internal issues. The months during which the family will experience chaos include the 3rd Chinese month (4 Apr. - 4 May.), the 6th Chinese month (6 Jul. - 6 Aug., the 8th Chinese month (7 Sep. - 7 Oct.), and the 10th Chinese month (7 Nov. - 5 Dec.) to increase care and attention to the health of people in the home and be careful of valuables being damaged or stolen.

Love

This year's love horoscope is characterized by waves and winds. Because you are quickly irritated, it leads to fights. Please be thoughtful and relaxed. Especially during the months when your love is quite fragile and it is easy to quarrel with each other, including the 3rd Chinese month (4 Apr. - 4 May), the 6th Chinese month (6 Jul. - 6 Aug.), the 8th Chinese month (7 Sep. - 7 Oct.) and 10th Chinese month (7

Nov. - 5 Dec.). Be wary of caustic phrases that may lead the other person to be offended or lose face. The second party arrives to add to the agony. Also, do not intervene or act as a third party in the relationships of others. Furthermore, be mindful of your behavior; being afflicted with sickness will catalyze unending squabbles.

Health

A good external criterion is the destiny owner's health. But darkness lurks inside. As a result, you must constantly monitor your body for irregularities, such as persistent discomfort in any place or discovering a lump that seems unnaturally large. You should consult a doctor right away for a checkup and treatment. If you wait too long, it will make therapy more difficult. You should also be more concerned about hygiene, drinking, and eating in a more sanitary manner. Especially during the following months, which are the 3rd Chinese month (4 Apr. - 4 May), the 6th Chinese month (6 Jul. - 6 Aug.), the 8th Chinese month (7 Sep. – 7 Oct.), and the 10th Chinese month (7 Nov. – 5

Dec.) Be careful of the danger of bleeding from accidents both during work and travel.

Year of the DOG (Gold) | (1958)

"The Dog naps during the day" is a person born in the year of the DOG at the age of 66 years (1958)

Overview

This age cycle is for the Year of the Dog horoscope since your zodiac sign this year will have a direct connection with the Year of the Dragon 2024. You will also have the ability to perform the annual royal homage to the gods. As a result, in every job activity, you must be more cautious and thoroughly examine the issue before proceeding. Some actions may necessitate some downtime. It is preferable to wait than to force oneself to do it and risk making mistakes and causing damage as a result. Perhaps you won't even get the opportunity to make amends. This is because there are three terrible stars in your horoscope this year: the Puenium star, the Huang Huang star, and the Xiao Ying star, all of which will hurt a variety of issues, including health issues, accidents, impediments, and employment troubles. There will be those near you who think dishonestly, malign you, or blame you. As a result, you should not trust anyone since you may come to regret it. However, there will be good fortune owing to poor luck in your lifetime. The fortunate stars "Hok Chae" (Happiness Star) and the Tee Koi Star (Earth Correction Star) will seem to shine in the middle of the year. Bright helps to diffuse and dispel some of the negative energy. But the Lord of Destiny must not forget to conduct good things and produce merit and merit. These two fortunate stars will boost generosity and help convert negative things into good.

Career and Business

This year has been a monsoon season in terms of work. Work will face challenges. In the commercial world, there will always be difficult difficulties to address. The job is exhausting, but the results are little and not worth the effort. Furthermore, you must be wary of internal agency tensions. Take caution not to cause errors or harm with your efforts. Signing contract paperwork necessitates extra vigilance. Especially during the following months that you cannot lack caution: the 3rd Chinese month (4 Apr. - 4 May.), the 6th Chinese month (6 Jul. - 6 Aug.), and the 8th Chinese month. (7 Sep. - 7 Oct.) and the 10th Chinese month (7 Nov. - 5 Dec.) Before investing in equities this year, you should think about it carefully. If you want to invest, you must carefully analyze your preparation and the money in your pocket to get extensive and comprehensive information. If you aren't ready yet or can't find it in time, the work will suffer as a result. You would have to postpone or cancel that task initially, rather than performing it halfway. In the middle, you must let your investment go to waste. However, within this year, there will be months in which your work and investments will turn around and improve, namely 1st Chinese Month (4 Feb. - 4 Mar.), the 2nd Chinese Month (5 Mar. - 3 Apr.), the 5th Chinese month (5 Jun. - 5 Jul.) and 9th Chinese month (8 Oct. - 6 Nov.)

Financial

The destined person's financial fortune will suffer a loss of wealth. When you receive a paycheck, you must manage your funds to handle any unexpected current needs that may arise. As a result, you should begin by spending as little as possible. Reduce needless expenses to avoid a shortage of money. Also, avoid being greedy to avoid falling victim to fraudsters. Gambling will not bring you any money. Especially during the months when your financial stars are down, including the 3rd Chinese month (4 Apr. - 4 May.), the 6th Chinese month (6 Jul. - 6 Aug.), the 8th Chinese month (7 Sep. – 7 Oct.), and the 10th Chinese month (7 Nov. – 5 Dec.) Do not let other people borrow money or sign any type of financial guarantee. As for the months in which your finances return to flowing smoothly, they are: 1st Chinese month (4 Feb. - 4 Mar.), the 2nd Chinese month (5 Mar. - 3 Apr.), the 5th Chinese month (5 Jun. - 5 Jul.) and the 9th Chinese month (8 Oct. - 6 Nov.).

Family

This year has been difficult for the family, with both internal and external occurrences causing concern. Members of the house regularly have problems and quarrels with neighbors. Forbidding or terminating certain matters does not mean that you are right without bias. As a result, you must be extremely mindful and calm. Be wary of harboring resentment as a result of issues that cannot be resolved, as this will result in suffering and damage. Especially during the months when troubles will occur in the family, namely the 3rd Chinese month (4 Apr. - 4 May.), the 6th Chinese month (6 Jul. - 6 Aug.), the 8th Chinese month (7 Sep. - 7 Oct.) and the 10th Chinese month (7 Nov. - 5 Dec.) Furthermore, you should be extra cautious about the safety and accidents that may occur to members of the household. Be wary of dishonest subordinates and items that have been destroyed or misplaced. Furthermore, you should avoid becoming involved in other people's conflicts, particularly litigation. Because you will be caught in the crossfire and will be forced to appear in court. The terrible months described above, in particular, should be avoided under exceptional circumstances.

Love

This year is neither wonderful nor poor in terms of love. If you are stuck and have a problem, your spouse or loved one will assist you in addressing numerous difficulties, or you may utilize this time to fix your bad luck and loss of cash. Instead, buy things and give them as gifts to your loved ones. It is sufficient to assist them or to take them on a trip, whether abroad or inside the nation, as suitable. It will assist in building the bond. However, you should be careful during the months when love is quite fragile and problems can easily occur, including the 3rd Chinese month (4 Apr. - 4 May), the 6th Chinese month (6 Jul. - 6 Aug.) 8th Chinese month (7 Sep. - 7 Oct.) and 10th Chinese month (7 Nov. - 5 Dec.) Words that must be carefully chosen will leave wounds in the listener's heart, causing troubles later on.

Health

This year is not going to be good for your physical health. Old ailments may reappear in old life. You should make time to rest. Be mindful of your diet. Food, especially sweet, greasy, and salty tastes, should be minimized, as should intoxicants such as whiskey, beer, and smoking. Especially during the month when your health might easily cause difficulties, such as needing to be more cautious about unforeseen mishaps. Including the 3rd Chinese month (4 Apr. - 4 May.), the 6th Chinese month (6 Jul. - 6 Aug.), the 8th Chinese month (7 Sep. - 7 Oct.), and the 10th Chinese month (7 Nov. - 5 Dec.) If you see anything strange, consult a doctor right away for an evaluation and treatment. If you leave it for too long, the sickness will spread and become tough to cure.

Year of the DOG (Gold) | (1970)

" The Dog is in morals. " is a person born in the year of the DOG at the age of 54 years (1970)

Overview

For individuals born in the Year of the Dog around the age of 54, this year is significant since your birth year is the year of battle (Chong) with the Year of the Dragon (2024), and your fate also has a direct impact on the Thai gods' yearly homage. Furthermore, this year's planets in your zodiac sign are Dao Sung Mung (star of grief), Dao Ung Huang, and Dao Phua Pai. All of this will have a detrimental impact on a variety of issues. Conflicts at both the high and lower levels of the organization, challenges and barriers at work and in business. This year, be cautious that trusting others too much can lead to bullying or being privately gossiped and slandered by those close to you who are dishonest. There is also an issue with the safety and health of the members of the household. Including the issue of financial liquidity, which is so limited that working capital is often in jeopardy. Problems with spouses and loved ones, who frequently bicker and argue over trivial topics and may suffer from bereavement for senior relatives. This year, therefore, you must be cautious of regulating every move you take. Increase your sobriety and tranquility before taking a step. Every activity must be carried out without carelessness.

Career and Business

This year's business work has been difficult. There is a strong likelihood that servants or subordinates will be untrustworthy or cause trouble. Both should be wary of internal and external disputes, as well as directives from superiors in their area of work. An unexpected move or additional job duties are possible. Especially during the 3rd Chinese month (4 Apr. - 4 May), the 6th Chinese month (6 Jul. - 6 Aug.), the 8th Chinese month (7 Sep. - 7 Oct. .), and the 10th month of China (7 Nov. - 5 Dec.) where you should be more cautious. When dealing with work, whether contracting for labor or employment, pay close attention to the smaller aspects. Be wary of being duped into losing a substantial quantity of money, as well as falling victim to fraudsters by mistake. This year, while making investments, you must apply your judgment rather than only focusing on rapid rewards since the consequences will cost you more than you earn.

The months in which your work and business will be smooth and bright include 1st Chinese month (4 Feb. - 4 Mar.), 2nd Chinese month (5 Mar. - 3 Apr.), 5th Chinese month. (5 Jun. – 5 Jul.) and the 9th Chinese month (8 Oct. – 6 Nov.).

Financial

With unpredictable revenue, this year's fortune-teller's financial fortunes will fluctuate. As a result, you must exercise caution while managing working capital, attempting to reserve liquidity and maintain enough reserves in the system. Because if you don't keep your costs under control, you will surely face a financial problem. Especially during the months when the financial stars are down and unexpected expenses may occur, such as the

3rd Chinese month (4 Apr. - 4 May), the 6th Chinese month (6 Jul. - 6 Aug.), the 8th Chinese month (7 Sep. - 7 Oct.) and the 10th Chinese month (7 Nov. - 5 Dec.) During these months, you should carefully arrange your budget and rigorously ban gaming. Take a risk or participate in criminal activity. This includes not allowing anyone to lend money or sign financial assurances. For the months when your finances will return to flowing smoothly, they are: 1st Chinese month (4 Feb. - 4 Mar.), 2nd Chinese month (5 Mar. - 3 Apr.), 5th Chinese month (5 June – 5 July) and the 9th Chinese month (8 Oct. – 6 Nov.).

Family

This year has not been kind to my family. Because this year, your birth year, is categorized as a poor year, which will result in home accidents, diseases of the elderly, and illnesses of persons in the home. Furthermore, there is the hardship of having a mourning norm for older relatives.

Including unexpected loss of property. During the months that there will be quite a lot of trouble within the family, they are the 3rd Chinese month (4 Apr. - 4 May), the 6th Chinese month (6 Jul. - 6 Aug.), the 8th Chinese month (7 Sep. - 7 Oct.) and the 10th Chinese month (7 Nov. - 5 Dec.) You should also be wary of disagreements between insiders and outsiders until they turn into a story. You should also be cautious of damaged goods. It was either stolen or the victim of a fraud. Relatives and friends are not permitted to intervene in other people's family disputes.

Love
The love horoscope for this year is volatile. Part of it is due to your emotions, which are both positive and negative at times. If you don't know how to manage your emotions, you can find yourself having to let go and walking in various ways. A third party will also be seen intervening in the middle. Arguments may develop if love lacks understanding, causing the fissures to spread and become more difficult to reconcile. Especially during the 3rd

Chinese month (4 Apr. - 4 May), the 6th Chinese month (6 Jul. - 6 Aug.), the 8th Chinese month (7 Sep. - 7 Oct. .) and the 10th Chinese month (7 Nov. - 5 Dec.) where you should avoid getting involved in other people's family matters. You should also avoid hanging out in entertainment venues. Be careful, you will find disease.

Health

This year's health is not looking good. What you must be cautious of are unforeseen mishaps, whether while working or relaxing. Including the danger of damage from travel accidents and a weaker body from lack of activity, resulting in a loss of immunity that can easily develop allergies and numerous infectious diseases. Especially during the months that your destiny must nourish your body and take special care of yourself, namely the 3rd Chinese month (4 Apr. - 4 May), the 6th Chinese month (6 Jul. - 6 Aug.), the 8th Chinese month (7 Sep - 7 Oct.) and the 10th Chinese month (Nov. 7 - Dec. 5). During this period, if you drink alcohol or other intoxicants, use public transportation. Do not drive. It will be safer by itself.

Year of the DOG (Water) | (1982)

" The Dog is out walking." is a person born in the year of the DOG at the age of 42 years (1982)

Overview

This age cycle is planned for the Year of the Dog. This is because the year of your birth is the year of the Thai god's annual offering as well as the Year of the Dragon (2024). Furthermore, several malevolent stars are congregating in your destiny to focus on and bother you. The hurdles become more obstructive than normal. As a result, at the start of the year, you should make time to pay respect to the Tai Suai deity to fend off ill luck and pray for benefits. To weaken the grip of misfortune. This year, you must constantly remind yourself not to be haughty, to forget yourself, and to be thoughtless. Because this year, three unfavorable stars will rule and affect you in your destiny house. Dao Sung Mueng (star of grief), Dao Pue Niam (star of wind), and Dao Ung Huang (star of vile strength) are among them. There are several things to be aware of and cautious of, such as safety issues and illnesses that may impact individuals in the house. Accidents can happen at work or when traveling. Be wary of the dangers of mourning for relatives and seniors, as well as being surreptitiously ruined in terms of reputation, honor, or influencing your professional position. Aside from the beginning of the year, an excellent strategy to fend against misfortune is to make time to pay reverence to the Tai Suai Buddha. This year, no job activity should be taken lightly.

Career and Business

This year will test your patience in terms of job and business. Some actions that take time necessitate waiting. Damage may occur if you are impatient or hasty. Both the operation of various activities must be mindful and meticulous so as not to make mistakes and create harm to return to solve old issues again and over. Especially during the months when work will falter and cause problems and obstacles, including the 3rd Chinese month (4 Apr. - 4 May), the 6th Chinese month (6 Jul. - 6 Aug.), the 8th Chinese month (7 Sep. - 7 Oct.)

and the 10th Chinese month (7 Nov. - 5 Dec.) Avoid investing in stocks, establishing a new career, and making other investments at this time. Furthermore, before signing any contract agreement, you must check over it thoroughly. Before signing, please read the tiny print. Otherwise, you'll have to fight for changes later. As for the months when work and trade will turn around and get better, they are: 1st Chinese month (4 Feb. - 4 Mar.), the 2nd Chinese month (5 Mar. - 3 Apr.), the 5th Chinese month (5 Jun. – 5 Jul.) and 9th Chinese month (8 Oct. – 6 Nov.).

Financial

This year's finances have been up and down, not consistent, with little income and big costs, so everything you can afford to save must be saved before searching for ways to improve your income. Don't overspend. Because you will be in a cash crisis several times during the year. Especially during the months when the financial stars are in decline, namely the 3rd Chinese month (4 Apr. - 4 May), the 6th Chinese month (6 Jul. - 6 Aug.), the 8th Chinese month

(7 Sep. – 7 Oct.) and the 10th Chinese month (7 Nov. – 5 Dec.) You should carefully manage your internal operating capital and avoid lending money to others or making financial commitments. Furthermore, one should not be greedy and expect to earn rich quickly by gambling or engaging in unlawful companies. To avoid property loss and being a victim of fraud. However, this year there are several months where you will have good luck with money, including 1st Chinese month (4 Feb. - 4 Mar.), 2nd Chinese month (5 Mar. - 3 Apr.), the 5th Chinese month (5 Jun. – 5 Jul) and 9th Chinese month (8 Oct. – 6 Nov.).

Family

This year, the family faced the malevolent stars Sung Mung and Huang Hw, who were circling to aim. You should be wary of health issues in your house, as well as confrontations between young people and neighbors. Including the risk of being slandered and slandered by those who do not want you well, as well as the risk of grief for aging relatives. Especially during the months when there will be chaos within the family, namely the 3rd Chinese month (4 Apr. - 4 May), the 6th Chinese month (6 Jul. - 6 Aug.), the 8th Chinese month (7 Sep. - 7 Oct.) and the 10th Chinese month (7 Nov. - 5 Dec.) You must improve home health care for the elderly and little children. This includes being cautious about valuables in the home being destroyed or stolen.

Love

The love horoscope for this year is not favorable. Those of you who have already lost a loved one. Be cautious, since there may be a change of heart. Part of this is due to your own heightened emotional volatility. The other portion will be triggered by a third party causing disruption. Those of you who are still unmarried this year must be cautious not to run into this issue unexpectedly. You must exercise strict self-control and avoid immorality and vices. Especially during the months that you need to be especially careful, including the 3rd Chinese month (4 Apr. - 4 May), the 6th Chinese month (6 Jul. - 6 Aug.), the 8th Chinese month (7 Sep. - 7 Oct.), and the

10th Chinese month (7 Nov. - 5 Dec.) Furthermore, you should not tamper with or intervene in the love lives of other people's relationships. You should also avoid acting recklessly and going out of your way.

Health

Your health is not excellent this year. Accidents that might occur while traveling or while driving should be avoided at all costs. You should also exercise caution if you interact with friends and consume alcohol. If you allow yourself to become so inebriated that you are unable to control yourself. There will be opportunities to injure yourself and others. The months in which you need to be careful of accidents and need to pay more attention to your health include the 3rd Chinese month (4 Apr. - 4 May.), the 6th Chinese month (6 Jul. - 6 Aug.), the 8th Chinese month (7 Sep. - 7 Oct.) and the 10th Chinese month (7 Nov. - 5 Dec.). If you observe any irregularities in your body during this period, you should consult a doctor right away for diagnosis and treatment so that symptoms may be treated as soon as possible.

Chinese Astrology Horoscope for Each Month

Month 12 in the Rabbit Year (6 Jan 23 - 3 Feb 23)

The horoscope draws towards a line of blocked energy as the year begins this month. As a result, there will be unexpected happenings and chaotic troubles at the start of the month that will never end. There are both harms and financial waste. What might assist in alleviating the situation is that you can limit the pattern of spending money this month by acquiring important products such as clothes, shoes, or supplies connected to creating a livelihood. In terms of work and business at this time, you must still be wary about minors causing difficulties and disagreements with coworkers. Be wary of being exploited as a scapegoat or having to take all responsibility for others.

This pay represents a loss of assets. Both had unanticipated bills that intervened. As a result, you should exercise strict control over how you spend your money. Also, do not lend money or sign financial assurances to anyone. This month is still not favorable for investing in stocks or making other types of investments; you should postpone it first.

The family's horoscope is concerned about losing money since they must care for individuals in the house and avoid mishaps. Be wary about having goods stolen or misplaced, or being a victim of fraudsters. As a result, you should be cautious and improve your home security. Relatives and friends should refrain from becoming engaged in legal conflicts. Because there might be repercussions.

In terms of love, there are no pros or downsides this month. Enough to keep the connection going through it.
Your horoscope for health: Because of excessive eating, be cautious of infectious infections. You should maintain good cleanliness, eat and live healthily, and get enough relaxation.

Support Days: 3 Jan., 7 Jan., 11 Jan., 15 Jan., 19 Jan., 23 Jan., 27 Jan., 31 Jan
Lucky Days: 4 Jan.,16 Jan., 28 Jan.
Misfortune Days: 5 Jan.,17 Jan., 29 Jan.
Bad Days: 8 Jan., 10 Jan., 20 Jan., 22 Jan.

Month 1 in the Dragon Year (4 Feb 23 - 5 Mar 23)
This month's destiny requirements for people born in the Year of the Dog have avoided the danger zone. The horoscope slope is upward, allowing you another chance to open your eyes and expand your wings. Work and business will discover ways to enhance some elements to fit into a better form. So, this month, keep your honesty to yourself. Various acts must be carried out with sincerity throughout this time. If you fake it, you'll be caught. Sincerity will assist you in overcoming challenges and troubles. You can turn negative things into positive ones.

This is a good starting pay. There was enough money to get by, but it was very short. As a result, please avoid incurring further debt, particularly by investing in windfalls through gambling or fortune telling, and avoid investing in new enterprises if you become engaged in investment stocks. There might be a loss of assets, resulting in a shortage of cash. Although the general direction of your work has altered for the better this month. However, it is still insufficient for new ventures. For the time being, you may only support the old one. You should not be sluggish. However, you must always establish strategies, budgets, and staff. So that when the time comes, you may proceed exactly as intended.

The family's wealth is stable, and elders will pay visits. This month is a wonderful opportunity for couples to sympathize, help, and share more.

Grilled foods are bad for your health. You should also avoid drinking alcohol and using drugs of any kind.

Support Days: 4 Feb., 8 Feb., 12 Feb., 16 Feb., 20 Feb., 24 Feb., 28 Feb.
Lucky Days: 9 Feb., 21 Feb.
Misfortune Days: 10 Feb., 22 Feb.

Bad Days: 1 Feb., 3 Feb., 13 Feb., 15 Feb., 25 Feb., 27 Feb

Month 2 in the Dragon Year (6 Mar 23 - 5 Apr 23)
This month's fate conditions for persons born in the Year of the Dog are still regarded favorable. The road to success arises abruptly because fortunate constellations appear to travel in orbit and glow brilliantly above the zodiac home. People will come in to promote or develop solutions to overcome issues in the workplace, including business. Overall, the task may progress smoothly, and success can be seen more clearly. This month, you should take advantage of the beautiful weather to continue working as usual. You will be able to quadruple your labor while still making money.

This pay fortune will bring in a lot of money. Cash inflows will come from a variety of sources, depending on what you have already invested. If you work hard, you will amass a great deal of riches. However, you should never stop learning and growing. You will find a method to earn from your investment.

Coordination in discussions will be seamless. Customers will assist businesses in making successful sales.

The family horoscope for this month is favorable. You will be able to greet elders who have traveled from other regions. The loving side is silky. Those of you who have a relationship should make an effort to meet in person regularly to ensure that the other person sympathizes with you. It is simpler to surrender to you.

In terms of health, you should still be cautious of the possibility of blood damage while traveling at this time. Even if mishaps from machines or sharp things occur, you cannot be careless.

New routes for joining into joint ventures or making other investments will be discovered. You may invest and expect a high return.

Support Days: 3 Mar, 7 Mar., 11 Mar., 15 Mar., 19 Mar., 23 Mar., 27 Mar., 31 Mar.
Lucky Days: 4 Mar, 16 Mar., 28 Mar
Misfortune Days: 5 Mar., 17 Mar., 29 Mar
Bad Days: 8 Mar, 10 Mar., 20 Mar., 22 Mar.

Month 3 in the Dragon Year (6 Apr 23 - 5 May 23)
This month marks the beginning of the Year of the Dragon, which is the Year of the Dragon. Every planned activity should be thoroughly considered before proceeding. Live life with mindfulness and patience. You cannot be impatient while solely using your emotions. This month, you may discover a chance to pay devotion to the Tai Suai Buddha to fend off ill luck and end the bad year. You and your family members will be safe. During this month, you should carefully organize your complete year's events. Investigate the preparedness of funds, work systems, and people. Plan work to accommodate people so that they can progress under their objectives.

There are still difficulties and issues in the corporate world, including internal disagreements. During this time, be cautious of being duped while signing contracts or engaging in joint ventures. Also, be wary of unexpected litigation or situations that may compel you to appear in court.

When revenue is consistent and begins to degrade, this wage is moderate in terms of fortune. As a result, you should not add to your financial load by investing in gambling, which is extremely dangerous. You should also not allow people to borrow money or sign any commitments.

The family side is tranquil. The members of the house love and respect one another.

This month is favorable for love and relationship horoscopes. It is possible to take your beloved on a journey to various locations to build and strengthen your love.

In terms of health, merely be cautious of infectious or contagious diseases, which are not very harmful.

This month is sufficient for starting a new work and making various investments. All you have to do is thoroughly study the material and don't put your confidence in others.

Support Days: 4 Apr., 8 Apr., 12 Apr., 16 Apr., 20 Apr., 24 Apr., 28 Apr.
Lucky Days: 9 Apr., 21 Apr.
Misfortune Days: 10 Apr., 22 Apr.
Bad Days: 1 Apr., 3 Apr., 13 Apr., 15 Apr., 25 Apr., 27 Apr.

Month 4 in the Dragon Year (6 May 23 - 5 Jun 23)
The fortunes of people born in the Year of the Dog are continuing to dwindle and not returning this month. Because the house of destiny has shifted and come into contact with a line of evil. You also get the deadly power of concentration from two malevolent stars, the Sung Mung star, and the Huang Huang star. Which extends its impact, only touching the negative side and creating harm. Obstacles and annoyance are reappearing to cause you more

trouble. You should also pay more attention to the health of others in your home. When driving or traveling, be cautious of accidents. You should not be reckless, including those who operate with machines. What you should do this month is learn how to take care of yourself and your family members by keeping them safe, which is called a precaution. Avoid activities or jobs that are unduly dangerous.

This month will witness a monsoon for labor and trade. Negotiating or organizing numerous activities will become difficult, and complications may arise. When signing numerous contracts at this time, be wary of being duped into being at a disadvantage. Furthermore, there will be disagreements inside the agency or organization. As a result, please take care of your tasks to the best of your ability.

In terms of money, this month represents a loss of fortune. You might fix the problem by purchasing items you want at the beginning of the month. Also, avoid gambling and making financial promises. This includes outlawing any enterprise that may violate the law. Horoscope for the family: Be wary of mishaps that may occur in the house, as well as the threat of thieves.

This month brings third-party winds that stir things up in the realm of love. It must be solid or there will be division.

Avoid getting involved in disagreements with family and friends.

Everything is not looking good for investing in numerous stocks this month. Everything seen is a deception.

Support Days: 2 May., 6 May., 10 May., 14 May., 18 May., 22 May., 26 May., 30 May
Lucky Days: 3 May., 15 May., 27 May.
Misfortune Days: 4 May., 16 May., 28 May.
Bad Days: 7 May., 9 May., 19 May., 21 May., 31 May.

Month 5 in the Dragon Year (6 Jun 23 - 6 Jul 23)

When the moon crosses the alliance line this month, smoothness begins to fade and impediments and issues reappear. What you should do on this occasion is to continue to support yourself, be alert, and thoroughly assess every topic before moving forward. When risking a significant investment, don't anticipate a tiny benefit. You must be cautious if you skip even one step in the game throughout this month. It might hurt the company's cash flow. During this phase of labor and business, both old and new challenges will be confronted front on.

Furthermore, there is the issue of people who disagree with one another, causing problems. Internal and foreign wars must be fought, and fair governance must be maintained. Don't pick what you like and ignore what you despise. Otherwise, hardworking workers would lose morale and drive.

This wage is modest in terms of wealth. Even though revenue is still pouring in from both regular jobs and supplementary money.

However, extravagant and arbitrary expenditure cannot be tolerated. You should also avoid gambling because it will be ineffective. Furthermore, this is another month in which you must be cautious of crooks. Keep an eye out for misplaced or stolen goods.

This month's family horoscope is not concerning because it is calm. In terms of love, it is sufficient to bring about happiness. If you are a single man looking for someone this month, please hurry up and ask; you will have hope. If you leave it for too long, whoever gets it first will be sorry.

Good health, but prevent injuries on the hands or legs and avoid alcohol and medication, which are all harmful. Because you are prone to sickness.

This month can be utilized to start new employment, enter stocks, and make other investments. Profits will be satisfactory in return.

Support Days: 3 Jun., 7 Jun., 9 Jun., 11 Jun., 15 Jun., 19 Jun., 23 Jun., 27 Jun.
Lucky Days: 8 Jun., 20 Jun.
Misfortune Days: 9 Jun., 21 Jun.
Bad Days: 2 Jun., 12 Jun., 14 Jun., 24 Jun., 26 Jun.

Month 6 in the Dragon Year (7 Jul 23 - 7 Aug 23)
This month, the journey to adulthood for people born in the Year of the Dog becomes more difficult. Because of a horrible month and being surrounded by a lot of bad stars. During this period, you should keep an eye on the security of your home. In particular, the disease of the elderly at home. Be wary of the hazards of bereavement for close senior relatives. Both financial horoscopes are still in a state of money decline. As a result, if you have time at the beginning of the month, you should find a way to honor the Buddha. You will receive blessings to help keep you and your family safe. The family is at peace and content.

Your profession and business will face challenges. Things that appear to be simple to pass have conditions. Without consideration, any activity might be reckless.

There will be unrest in the house if the family's circumstances do not improve. People's sicknesses in the house, accidents, and youngsters generate continuous bother and turmoil.

There were disagreements about love and relationships. To obtain an agreement, you must regulate your thinking and remain cool when speaking. In terms of financial luck, bad luck will cause you to lose your riches. Be wary of unforeseen charges that can quickly pile up.

Your health is deteriorating. Be cautious of mishaps that may result in bleeding, particularly at work and when traveling.

In terms of family and friends, you should avoid relatives who prefer to invite you down the path of vice or those who manufacture dream imagery to deceive you into giving them money during this time.

This month is not promising in terms of collaboration and investment. To be safe, you should avoid it.

Support Days: 1 Jul., 5 Jul., 9 Jul., 13 Jul., 17 Jul., 21 Jul., 25 Jul., 29 Jul.
Lucky Days: 2 Jul., 14 Jul., 26 Jul.
Misfortune Days: 3 Jul., 15 Jul., 27 Jul.
Bad Days: 6 Jul., 8 Jul., 18 Jul., 20 Jul., 30 Jul.

Month 7 in the Dragon Year (8 Aug 23 - 7 Sep 23)
As we begin this new month, we have come through many challenging months. The fate conditions have been altered to include the month in which the Sompong is an ally. An auspicious star was also circling in and shining brightly. The long-awaited road to success has finally been revealed. Careers and enterprises demonstrate their smoothness and radiance. Many things were accomplished as a result of our being stranded and in a crisis. Someone will be there to assist and advise. As a result, during this month, you should utilize the correct individuals for the proper work. It will double the results. You must also know how to grasp

golden chances and invest in items for which you are prepared and have information. Mobilize already planned and prepared plans and money. Please get it out and make good use of it this month. Because you'll meet individuals with experience who will encourage and assist you. As a result, there will be more power to go forward than previously.

There is a lot of money on the other side of this pay fortune. There will be revenue coming in from a variety of sources. Make careful to set aside money for emergencies. During this time, there is calm among the family, and favorable energy has come to visit. People in the home will get excellent news. Both members adore and respect one another. Be happier and more cheerful.

This is a good time for your health. There was nothing to be concerned about in terms of major ailments.

It is a particularly attractive period for love. You have a good chance of success if you study and are in a relationship.

This month is favorable for family and friends. If you have an issue, you will be assisted.

It is feasible to invest both within and outside the firm this month if you start working in joint ventures or invest in diverse industries.

Support Days: 2 Aug., 6 Aug., 10 Aug., 14 Aug., 18 Aug., 22 Aug., 26 Aug., 30 Aug.

Lucky Days: 7 Aug., 19 Aug., 31 Aug.
Misfortune Days: 8 Aug., 20 Aug.
Bad Days: 1 Aug., 11 Aug., 13 Aug., 23 Aug., 25 Aug.

Month 8 in the Dragon Year (8 Sep 23 - 7 Oct 23) The horoscope curve has struck a snag this month. Because the house of fate faced clashing strength from a group of wicked stars. As a result, you will encounter minors in the workplace who are considering corruption and embezzlement and may be slandered and slandered. As a result, each action must fill in the gaps; don't be casual. This month, you should focus on controlling your emotions and words. Because you tend to mock and taunt, be cautious of some remarks that may offend others. It was never an issue previously. However, this month, avoid carrying grudges and plotting revenge on the other person.

In terms of work and business this month, be aware of events changing abruptly into another concern. Those who work full time, be careful about transferring and changing positions. Those in business should be wary of disagreements or misunderstandings with customers or coworkers. Also, keep in mind that rash decisions will lead to mistakes in your own business.

It's a criterion in terms of money: receive a little, pay a lot. Be wary of the lack of liquidity in the system's money. As a result, you should not gamble or invest in anything that might lead to disobeying the law or abusing the rights of others.

The family fortune is serene and orderly. However, on the love front, we frequently encounter unhappiness and disagreements. As a result, you should practice more patience and composure.

Finding time to exercise to improve your body's immune system can aid if your health horoscope experiences small ailments. During this time, families and friends must be careful not to get insulted by remarks that do not make sense to each other. As a result, you should avoid disputes and disagreements. This will not cause the situation to worsen.

Starting a new career, buying stocks, and making other investments are still difficult.

Support Days: 3 Sep, 7 Sep., 11 Sep, 15 Sep, 19 Sep., 23 Sep., 27 Sep..
Lucky Days: 12 Sep, 24 Sep.
Misfortune Days: 13 Sep, 25 Sep.
Bad Days: 4 Sep, 6 Sep., 16 Sep, 18 Sep, 28 Sep., 30 Sep.

Month 9 in the Dragon Year (8 Oct 23 - 6 Nov 23)

Even those born in the Year of the Dog will see their fortunes improve as the month progresses. However, the accumulated work difficulties from the previous era have not been resolved. As a result, you must continue to attempt to improve your diligence. Always strive to improve yourself and your job to stay up with changing situations. Don't be a slacker. However, we must act promptly to identify the root cause and resolve the resulting issues. This month, you should remember that where you put effort, there will be success. Your investment during this time will not be squandered; rather, it will accrue and be returned to you later.

It will have a beneficial influence throughout this period if the trading trend is steady and developing. As a result, you should visit your consumers frequently to create and sustain solid connections. Furthermore, you can build on previous foundations, develop new ones, or enhance outside investment this month. The future will take a positive turn.

This pay is regarded to be in good shape in terms of good fortune, with money coming in. However, there is no luck in gaming this month, so don't get your expectations up. If you are preoccupied with investing, you will dive too deep and never recover.

The fortunes of the family are serene, and favorable energy appears to wash the dwelling. As a result, the chosen individual is likely to move into a new house or domicile or to experience other auspicious occurrences in the house.

In terms of relationships, there will be more mutual support during this time, and you will meet someone you love who will collaborate with you better in every way.

In terms of health, even if the outside appears to be in good shape, one must be wary of reoccurring ailments such as diabetes and high blood pressure. If you see any changes in your body, you should consult a doctor right away.

This month, there will be people pointing out new methods to invest in various investments. You can invest according to your abilities.

Support Days: 1 Oct., 5 Oct., 9 Oct., 13 Oct., 17 Oct., 21 Oct., 25 Oct., 29 Oct.
Lucky Days: 6 Oct., 18 Oct., 30 Oct.
Misfortune Days: 7 Oct., 19 Oct., 31 Oct.
Bad Days: 10 Oct., 12 Oct., 22 Oct., 24 Oct.

Month 10 in the Dragon Year (7 Nov 23 - 6 Dec 23)

This month, the route of your life twists and turns, and your destiny collides. As a result, the road of destiny varies downhill, with barriers, challenges, and contradictions all appearing gradually. This month, you should assist your job in your obligations to the best of your ability. Interfere with no one else's task. Furthermore, you should hurry to clean up any work that has been left behind so that it does not gather as dirt and cover the pig's tail. It will just bring you more difficulty.

This pay appears to have exposed asset loss points. Allow no one to borrow money or sign financial assurances as a result. You will face a lawsuit if you bet or get involved in crooked trading, tax evasion, or criminal activities.

Workplace disagreements and issues persisted at both the higher and lower levels of management. Signing certification in various contract documents necessitates extensive information verification.

Families should be wary of burglars entering into their assets' homes this month. You should keep them hidden and take special precautions to avoid harm. You should be vigilant and avoid falling victim to fraudsters. In addition, be wary of persons in your neighborhood who are bickering or disputing with one other.

When it comes to love, you must be cautious while expressing strong feelings, since this will result in a bitter dispute. You should also be respectful and refrain from going to places of amusement. Be cautious of allergies, colds, and seasonal infectious disorders.

In terms of family and friends, we must be wary of the wolf in sheep's clothing this month. Don't put your confidence in anyone. When it comes to teamwork or investing, be wary of being duped into losing your money.

Support Days: 2 Nov., 6 Nov., 10 Nov., 14 Nov., 18 Nov., 22 Nov., 26 Nov., 30 Nov
Lucky Days: 11 Nov., 23 Nov.
Misfortune Days: 12 Nov., 24 Nov.
Bad Days: 3 Nov., 5 Nov., 15 Nov., 17 Nov., 27 Nov., 29 Nov.

Month 11 in the Dragon Year (7 Dec 23 - 5 Jan 24)
This month's destiny criteria have shifted into a favorable month, helping your destiny curve to grow more buoyant and soar. Obstacles and troubles fade away with time. It is said to be the last month of the year as a gift of inspiration to you. As a result, you should examine the preparedness of both labor and financial resources to spend this month. In addition,

consider the auspicious moment and appropriate opportunity, and then go in and maximize your potential. Accelerate the generation of outcomes, produce sales, increase money, and increase production capacity to grow. When the tide rises, it is necessary to move quickly and scoop it up to make progress and regain market leadership.

This pay fortune is abundant; money comes in and grows. Direct cash flow and money from investments in many places that will grow and rise for you to be pleased are both sources of income. In terms of job, you might be able to locate a benefactor to assist you. The commercial business is progressing well, and all activities are flowing more smoothly and conveniently. Customers will obey your requests if you do business, making it simple to purchase and sell.

This is another month of good energy within the family. People in the home will hear excellent news, or you may have the opportunity to welcome new members.

The road of love is straightforward and comfortable. If you dare to ask for the other person's affection, you venture to make a choice.

Despite his good health, he is concerned about driving on the road. As a result, it should not be undervalued. You should not drive if you have consumed alcohol or other intoxicants.

This month's horoscope for relatives and friends. Even if you find nice goods, what you acquire from friends should be considered. You may not receive it again if you do not show consideration and moderation.

Starting a new job, investing in stocks, and making other investments this month are all considered positive moves, with investors looking for a good return.

Support Days: 4 Dec., 8 Dec., 12 Dec., 16 Dec., 20 Dec., 24 Dec., 28 Dec.
Lucky Days: 5 Dec., 17 Dec., 29 Dec
Misfortune Days: 6 Dec., 18 Dec., 30 Dec

Bad Days: 9 Dec., 11 Dec., 21 Dec., 23 Dec.

Amulet for The Year of the Dog
"Cai Shen | God of wealth."

This year, those born in the Year of the Dog should set up and revere spiritual things. "Cai Shen Pair of Millionaires Grants Wealth" to improve your fortune by setting it on your work desk or cash register and asking for His aid in promoting the fortune-teller's business and trade smoothly and prospering. All year long, the family is content and safe.

A chapter in the Department of Advanced Feng Shui discusses the gods who will come to reside in the mia keng (house of destiny) for the year. They are gods capable of bringing both good and terrible fortune to the god of fate in that year. When this is the case, worship will improve your luck with the gods that visit you on your birthday. As a consequence, it is said to produce positive benefits and have the most impact on you. To relied on god's power to protect him when his fortunes declined and his miseries were lessened. At the same time, you are blessed with a smooth company operation and your dreams are granted, giving you and your family riches and prosperity.

Those born in the year of the dog or Mia Keng (destiny home) belong to the zodiac sign Suk. Because the year of his birth offended the Tai Suai deity. It also falls during the Year of the Dragon, 2024. This year, job and finances have been up and down, swinging between good and dismal. There is a lot of competition out there. As a result, you must use extreme caution in any financial transactions. There is a paucity of liquidity. Many issues have the potential to take unexpected turns.

You should avoid engaging in illicit activities or infringing on intellectual property rights. You must attempt to be more patient and tolerant in love. They may divorce because they frequently dispute over irrelevant issues. In terms of health, he is irritated and unpleasant. You must take care of your mental health for your body to remain healthy. If you wish to solve the competing energy problem, you should put up a sacred item and wear an auspicious pendant. "Cai Shen Pair of Millionaires Grants Wealth," she says, requesting power and status from him. Help preserve your destiny from tragedy, boost business success and wealth, and provide you and your family peace and happiness.

"Cai Shen Pair of Millionaires Grants Wealth" They were both dressed in full Chinese noble robes, with endless rich diamonds decorating their brows. The first has a chunk of gold in one hand, which represents affluence. His other hand was holding the Yu Yi staff, a sign of authority, distinction, and honor. The second individual had an auspicious sign that said "Cai Shen Tao," which implies that the god Chai Xing Yea has come to visit your home. The two Chai Xing deities appeared to bless the deities of the Year of the Dog. This is because the fortune of the Year of the Dog this year is a source of leakage and financial loss. As a result, unforeseen costs will frequently interfere, causing property loss and disturbing serenity. As a result, if you worship "Cai Shen Pair of Millionaires Grants Wealth" to improve their fortunes. It will help you have a successful career. Business is thriving, and family life is harmonious. It also improves working capital liquidity and ensures that money flows smoothly and without interruption.

Those born in the Year of the Dog should also wear an auspicious pendant. "Cai Shen Pair of Millionaires Grants Wealth" to wear around your neck or carry with you when traveling both near and far away from home. Prosperity and growth in commerce and trade are required for the owner of his destiny to be filled with money and auspicious places. All year, the family is tranquil and joyful. It generates greater and faster efficiency and effectiveness than previously.

Good Direction: Northeast, East, and South
Bad Direction: Southwest
Lucky Colors: Red, Pink, Orange, White, and Silver.
Lucky Times: 3.00 – 06.59, 11.00 – 12.59, 19.00 – 20.59.

Bad Times: 07.00 – 08.59, 13.00 – 14.59., 17.00 – 18.59

Good Luck For 2024

Printed in Great Britain
by Amazon